THE ANGRY DRAGON

by Michael Gordon

THIS BOOK BELONGS TO

....

....

It was time for George and his pet dragon, Joe, to play.

With all their toys spread out, they were having a fun day

Until George accidentally broke Joe's favorite toy.

"Look what you've done!" Joe yelled, "You silly boy!"

Joe flew into a rage. He got angry and red.

"It was an accident," a sorry George said.

"I'm sorry I've upset you. Let's talk it out.

Don't be so angry. You don't have to shout."

"Breathe deeply and let's talk about how you feel.

We can fix the toy. It's really not a big deal."

Joe breathed and felt better. George was right.

He loved his best friend, and he didn't want to fight.

George helped Joe fix his toy with Dad's glue.

Before long, it was as good as new.

That afternoon, George was helping his mom clean.

Joe wanted him to play. He thought George was being mean.

Feeling hurt, Joe called George
a very horrible name.

He said, "You're not my friend
if you won't play my game."

George breathed deeply and
said, "Joe, please don't be mad.

Be patient and wait for me.
There's no need to feel bad."

"There's time to help Mom
and have fun too.

You're my best buddy, Joe.
I will play with you."

Joe listened to his friend and
waited until George was done.

Then they played music
together and had lots of fun.

They were hungry in the
kitchen later that day.

Joe wanted to eat lots of sweets.
George said, "No way!

Eating lots of sweets is bad for
your teeth and tummy too."

Joe yelled, "I'll eat what I want!
Don't tell me what to do!"

Joe ate all of the sweets
and then later that night,

He complained that his
tummy didn't feel right.

He needed to lie down. He
felt so horrible and sad.

"I'm sorry I didn't listen to
you," Joe said, "I feel bad."

"Getting my way hasn't turned out very well," Joe said.

As George helped him sip water while he lay in bed.

George took care of his friend. He wanted Joe to feel good.

He did everything for Joe that a best friend should.

"I'm going to be more patient and less greedy," Joe said.

"And instead of getting angry, I'll try talking to you instead."

"That's great. I'm proud of you," George said to his friend.

The boys laughed and chatted until the day came to an end.

About author

Michael Gordon is the talented author of several highly rated children's books including the popular Sleep Tight, Little Monster, and the Animal Bedtime.

He collaborates with the renowned Kids Book Book that creates picture books for all of ages to enjoy. Michael's goal is to create books that are engaging, funny, and inspirational for children of all ages and their parents.

Contact

For all other questions about books or author,
please e-mail michaelgordonclub@gmail.com.

Award-winning books

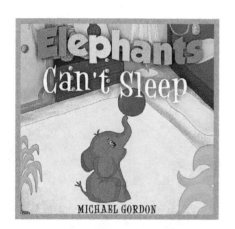

Elephants Can not Sleep

The

Little Elephant likes to break the rules. He never cleans his room. He never listens to mama's bedtime stories and goes to bed really late. But what if he tried to follow the routine so that the bedtime would become an amazing experience?

Little Girl's Daddy

the Who Needs a super hero the when you have your dad? Written in beautiful rhyme this is an excellent story that honors all fathers in the world.

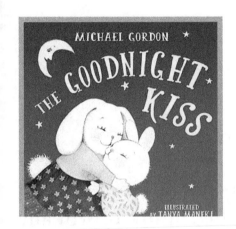

The Goodnight Kiss

Welcome to a cozy, sweet little bunny family. Mom is putting her little son Ben to bed, but she's not quite successful. Little boy still wants to play games and stay up late. Ben also likes to keep his mommy in his room at bedtime. Mrs. Bunny tries milk, warm blankets, books , and finally a kiss ... what will work?

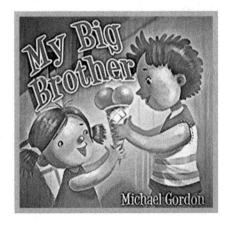

My Big Brother

The

Each of our lives will always be a special part of the other. There's Nothing Quite Like A Sibling Bond Written in beautiful rhyme this is an excellent story that values patience, acceptance and bond between a brother and his sister.

Thank You!

For purchasing this book,

I'd like to give you a free gift

An amazing bedtime story for your child

https://michaelgordonclub.wixsite.com/books

CPSIA information can be obtained
at www.ICGtesting.com
Printed in the USA
BVHW050138240120
570304BV00001B/4